GAMES
FROM MANY
LANDS

GAMES FROM MANY LANDS

BY ANITA BENARDE

A LION BOOK

To Scott, Andi and Dana
and their friends everywhere —

and also to Mel.

Copyright © 1970 by Anita Benarde
Published by Sayre Publishing, Inc.
52 Park Avenue, New York, N.Y. 10016
All rights reserved
Published simultaneously in Canada by George J. McLeod, Ltd.
73 Bathurst Street, Toronto 2B, Ontario
ISBN: 0-87460-081-2; Libr. ed: 0-87460-147-9
Library of Congress Catalog Card Number: 71-86975
This book was printed and bound in the United States of America
2nd Printing

CONTENTS

Foreword, Mary Winskill 7
Introduction 9
Snow Football, *Alaska* 10
Trick the Dancers, *American Indian* 12
Drop the Marble, *Central America* 14
Chase the Dragon's Tail, *China* 16
Beware the Antelope, *The Congo* 20
The Whales, *Denmark* 22
Scotland Yard, *England* 24
Swap Chairs—by the Numbers, *France* 26
Unwrap the Chocolate, *Germany* 28
The Fishermen, *Ghana* 30
Catch the Cap, *Guatemala* 32
Windmill, *Holland* 34
Balancing Toys, *India* 38
Pass the Orange, *Ireland* 40
Hold the Rope, *Israel* 42
Tug O' War, *Korea* 44
Stick Games, *New Zealand* 46
Cat and Mice, *Philippine Islands* 48
Hit the Stones, *Portugal* 50
Bell in the Steeple, *Russia* 52
Hit the Holes, *Saudi Arabia* 56
Name the Animal, *Switzerland* 58
Kukla, *Turkey* 60
About the author-illustrator 63

FOREWORD

As a teacher, I have had the rare good fortune to help educate children from many different countries. I have learned in the classroom that capacities and appetites for education vary from individual to individual. Most students fling themselves joyfully into their studies.

Although children may have widely varying national and ethnic backgrounds, they do have a common meeting ground in the games they play. In this book are popular games from many countries of the world. It is in game playing that children learn about fair play and sportsmanship, and the values of working together in a group. In games, the importance of coordinating the mind with the physical strengths of the body is realized. Perhaps most important of all, a child learns to know himself while playing games with others. By knowing himself, by discovering his own strengths and weaknesses, a child has taken a first step toward knowing and liking and loving others. That's what game playing—and life itself— is all about.

Mary Winskill
New York, New York

7

INTRODUCTION

Why do children play games? Probably the main reason is for sheer enjoyment. They play because it's fun. The games in this book were selected because they appeared to be games that children all over the world would enjoy. Most of the games do not require special equipment, or if equipment is needed, it is the kind that is almost universally available. Stones or marbles, a length of rope, a tin can are some of the materials used in our games. As often as not, though, a stick to draw a goal line is all one needs—plus, of course, a healthy imagination, something most children have in abundance.

Enjoyment of a game usually is ample reward for a child. But he gets a great deal more than that. Strength and stamina and grace are some by-products. Getting along with others and teamwork are learned. And since there often are more losers than winners, a child discovers the art of losing gracefully and winning modestly.

This book tells children just a little about games that are played in other countries. And in playing these games, perhaps they will learn—as the author did in selecting the games—that foreign games suddenly seem very familiar. The longer a child plays a game, the more familiar it becomes. And the more a group of children play together, the more each individual likes every other individual.

SNOW FOOTBALL □ Alaska, U.S.A.

Eskimo children play this game on hard-packed snow in the winter. But it can be played almost anywhere. They use a leather pouch stuffed with moss or animal hair, but a basketball, volleyball or football can be substituted.

This game is really more like European soccer than American football. The object is to kick the ball over the goal line of the opposing team.

Two goals are drawn in the snow about 70 feet apart. The players elect two captains who, in turn, choose their teams. The teams line up on the goal lines, facing each other.

The ball is placed on the ground in the exact center of the field between the two goal lines. At a shout from one of the captains, both teams leave the goal lines and rush for the ball. The team which knocks the ball through the opponent's goal wins the game.

Usually some players fall back toward their goal and try to keep the other team from kicking the ball past their goal line. Before the game starts the teams decide on the size of the goals. If a goal is four feet wide, it is easy to kick the ball through, but not impossible to defend.

If you want to play this game, you may want to substitute a large cardboard box for a goal drawn on the ground. By using a box, there can be no argument about when a goal is scored.

TRICK THE DANCERS □ American Indian

Indian children from many of the tribes on the northwest coast of the United States used to play this game, which is a different kind of musical chairs. A drummer beats on his drum while the dancers dance. But when the drummer stops, so must the dancers.

Not one step may be taken after the drum stops. This often leaves the dancers in awkward positions. One may have a foot high in the air. Another may be crouched down or ready to jump.

Sometimes the drummer is hidden from the dancers. But most of the time he is in the center of a circle. As the drummer begins, the boys and girls dance slowly around him. The longer the music continues, the faster the drummer plays. Sometimes he varies the music from fast to slow, and the dancers must keep time to the beat.

When the music stops, so do the dancers. They must freeze, even if the tricky drummer stops at an inconvenient moment. The dancers still in motion when the music stops must leave the circle. They become watchers.

After the players who didn't stop dancing in time leave the circle, the drummer starts over. And the dancers begin again. One by one they make mistakes, until finally only one dancer remains. He is the winner and becomes the drummer for the next game.

This game is fun even without a real drum. You can use an old gallon can or any instrument that the drummer can beat to make music.

DROP THE MARBLE □ Central America

Children in Central and South America love games of skill. One game, for two players, is played with marbles—or stones—and pits one individual's skills against another's. The winner of this game ends up with all the marbles.

Each player begins with five marbles. The two contestants first toss a marble at a line they draw on the ground. The player whose marble falls closest to the line begins.

The two players face each other. The winner of the toss stands at attention, heels together and toes spread wide. The second player crouches about five feet away. He tosses a marble toward the spread toes of the other. If he fails to land a marble between the toes and heels in three chances, he loses one marble.

But, if the second player succeeds in placing a marble between the heels and the toes, the standing player drops one of his marbles. The first player may look down, but he must stand straight. He drops the marble from the height of his waist. If he hits his opponent's marble, he wins the marble. If he misses, he loses the marble, and forfeits his own marble to his opponent.

In the second game, the players change places—one tossing a marble and the other spreading his feet, but with his heels together. The contest is over when one player owns all the marbles.

An interesting variation is a team game. First two leaders are chosen. They in turn pick their teams. The team that owns the most marbles after half an hour wins the game.

CHASE THE DRAGON'S TAIL □ China

Folk tales of many countries the world over recall the days of huge, fire-breathing reptiles. These fearsome creatures were called dragons. They guarded hidden treasures, carried off fair maidens and destroyed farmer's crops with their fiery breath.

Dragon legends are still told in China. Paper dragons march in Chinese parades. And the Chinese children play the old, old game of catching the dragon's tail. The game is simple, but no one has an easy time catching the tail.

The players line up one behind the other. The boy or girl at the front of the line is called the head. The player at the end is the tail. The head runs in a big circle, trying to catch the tail. Why is it so hard to catch the dragon's tail? Because (see illustration) each player puts his arms on the shoulders of the player in front of him. The line of players actually becomes a dragon that twists and turns and does everything it can to keep the head from catching the tail.

The more players there are, the more fun. When the head manages to catch the tail, the head drops out of the line. In his place goes the old tail (the person who was at the end of the line). The new head then tries to catch the new tail. And all the time the body of the dragon squirms and wiggles and tries to keep the head from touching the tail. But the players must be careful not to break the line. Every time a head catches a tail the line becomes shorter. The game is over when only two players are left.

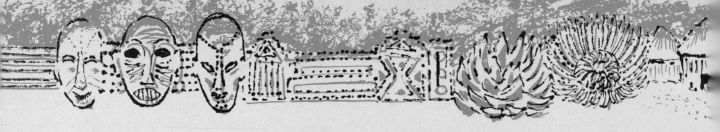

BEWARE THE ANTELOPE □ The Congo

Antelopes—even the small antelopes of Africa—are surefooted and can run very fast. This is good, for many other animals like to hunt the antelope for food, and he must be swift to escape.

The Luba Kasai children of the Congo play a tag game. The leader is called the antelope. Before the game begins, a square or oblong field is drawn, or the exact boundaries are somehow determined. As the game starts, the antelope is in the center and the other players stand around the edges of the square.

Now comes the switch. Instead of the others chasing the antelope, he runs after them. If he tags another player, or if a player runs outside the boundaries, this player also becomes an antelope. Then the tagged players help to tag the others.

Usually the game is fast, and doesn't often last long. The last player to be tagged is the winner of the game. The winner gets to be the antelope for the second game.

THE WHALES □ Denmark

Danish men have always been great sailors. One popular game reflects the Danes' interest in the sea. All players pair off for a kind of musical chairs.

One of the couples is named to lead the game; these two are called whales. The other couples find seats together anywhere in the room. Then each couple selects a name of a fish, writes it on a slip of paper and hands it to the whales.

The whales begin to walk hand in hand around the room. Weaving in and out among the couples' chairs, they start to call out the names of the fish on the slips of paper.

"Barracuda," they shout. And, "herring, dolphin and tuna!"

Any couple that has selected one of these names rises when the name is called. Then they fall in behind the whales, still marching around the room.

After the whales have called out all the names and every couple is marching around the room, the whales call out: "A storm is coming; head for home!"

All of the players marching behind the whales run for seats. The couples cannot separate; they must stay in pairs and find seats together. The whales know when the game is about to end, of course, and seldom have any trouble finding seats. The couple unable to find chairs will be the whales for the next game. For each game all couples select a new name.

SCOTLAND YARD □ England

This is a popular game in England, where it is also called "Detective" or "Murder." A slip of paper for each player in the game goes into a hat. Most of these slips have the word "witness" written on them. Two of the slips are different: One will say "detective," and the other, "the killer."

The hat is passed around. Everyone draws a slip. The detective identifies himself and leaves the room. The killer tells the witnesses who he is. Then the detective returns, takes a seat and the lights are turned off.

All players but the detective are free to move around. When the killer tags someone in the dark, the victim screams. A few seconds later the lights go on again. (One person should be appointed to turn lights on and off.)

The detective must find out who the killer is. He can question any player. (You should decide before the game begins how many questions the detective is allowed.) The murdered person, of course, is dead and cannot answer. The killer may lie, but the witnesses must tell the truth.

However, the detective may not ask directly who the killer is. But he may ask a different question of each witness: "Where were you standing in the room?" "Did you hear a noise nearby?" "To the right or the left?"

Finally, after the detective has asked all his questions, he asks one more—a question that he may ask just once: "Did you kill the victim?" He asks this question only of one person, and this query is the only one that the killer must answer truthfully. If the answer to this final question is "no," the detective is fired. If the answer is "yes," the detective has solved the mystery and is the winner. Then the slips go back into the hat, are drawn again and a new detective gets his chance to solve a murder.

A deck of playing cards may be substituted for the slips of paper. The player who picks the ace of spades becomes the murderer and the jack of hearts designates the detective. The players who pick the other cards are the witnesses.

SWAP CHAIRS - BY THE NUMBERS □ France

This amusing French game is an alternate way to play Blind Man's Bluff, a favorite in some form in many countries of the world. In the French version, all players but one sit in chairs in a circle. The one player not sitting down picks one of the players in the circle and begins there. He asks the children to count in turn. The number each child calls out is his number, and everyone must remember his own, even if he has to write it down. Then the standing player is blindfolded.

The game starts with the blindfolded player standing in the middle of the circle. He calls out two numbers, perhaps 2 and 25. Players with

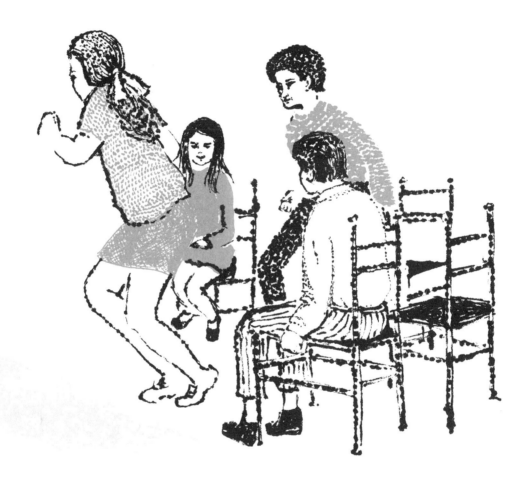

these numbers must exchange seats. The object of the game is for the blindfolded player either to catch a player, or to find a seat left vacant during an exchange.

No player may slip outside the circle. He may walk or crawl as quietly as possible while the others are swapping chairs. Once the game has started, the blindfolded player may move anywhere inside the circle— but not outside.

When the blindfolded player tags someone, he takes his number and seat. The tagged player then is blindfolded, and the game continues.

UNWRAP THE CHOCOLATE □ Germany

Winners of this German game get an immediate reward—a bite of chocolate. Any number can play the game, but it's more fun if not more than eight sit around the table playing.

You will need a thick chocolate bar, a hat, a scarf, a pair of gloves, a knife, a fork and a pair of dice. All of these are piled in the middle of the table.

Before the game actually starts, everyone rolls the dice. The high number determines who rolls first when the game begins. Once the starter has been decided, he rolls the dice.

If he throws a double number—ones, twos, threes, fours, fives or sixes—he quickly puts on the hat, gloves and scarf and begins to unwrap the chocolate bar. The bar has been wrapped in newspapers or in several layers of heavy brown paper.

Meanwhile, the dice have been passed to the leader's right and the next person rolls. If he gets a double, he puts on the hat, scarf and gloves and continues to unwrap the chocolate. If he doesn't get a double, he passes the dice to his right. Everyone has a chance to roll the dice, and often the dice are passed quickly around the table without anyone throwing a double.

The object of the game is to get the chocolate unwrapped. Then with the knife and fork, the person wearing the hat, scarf and gloves, can cut off a piece of the bar and eat it. If, however, he does not have the chocolate in his mouth when another player rolls a double, he must stop and pass the props on to that player.

What usually happens in that several persons will help unwrap the chocolate, but only one player will get a bite. After someone takes a bite of chocolate, the game stops while the chocolate bar is rewrapped in several layers of paper. Then the game starts over. When all the chocolate is eaten, the game is finished.

THE FISHERMEN □ Ghana

The children of Ghana enjoy this game of make-believe. Before they start, the players draw lines on the ground to set definite limits. They may draw a circle, a square, or a rectangle; whatever the shape of the boundaries, the area inside represents a lake or a river in which fish may swim.

Once the fishing area has been established, the group selects four boys or girls to be the fishermen. The fishermen have one piece of equipment—a rope. They pretend that this rope is a net for catching fish.

When the game starts, most of the players are running around inside the boundaries, pretending they are fish swimming. The fishermen grasp the rope and act as if they were wading into the water. They chant a song as they go. Any song you like will do, as long as everyone can sing along. As the last words are sung, the fishermen try to surround as many fish as possible with the rope.

Those caught inside the rope at the end of the song are out of the game. The fish can escape the "net" by running to the boundary lines so that the fishermen can't get behind them.

When the game starts the second time, all the fish who have been caught become fishermen. They try to help catch the fish still swimming in the water. The game is over when all the fish have been roped in by the fishermen. The last four fish to be caught will be the fishermen in the next game.

CATCH THE CAP □ Guatemala

Guatemalan children carve a skill game from an empty thread spool. They call it *Capirucho*—catch the cap. They attach a string and a long peg to the spool. The idea is to toss the carved spool into the air and stick the peg into the hole, which has been rounded out. Try your hand at making this. You may want to use a small block of white pine, rather than an old spool, since pine is easy to carve. Here's how:

1. Start with an empty spool or wooden block.
2. Smoothly round off one end. Leave the other end flat, but cut a large depression on the flat end, which makes it easier for the peg to slide into the hole.
3. Cut out part of the body about one-third of the way up the spool from the flat end.
4. Paint or decorate to your own taste.
5. Knot string. With a needle draw it through a small piece of heavy leather or cloth. Glue this cloth or leather to the rounded end.
6. Sharpen stick to a point and tie string to unsharpened end. This peg should be about 2 inches long. The string should be about 9 inches long.
7. See if you can catch the cap!

There are many variations of this skill game around the world. In France (see drawing) children use a wooden ball about the size of a croquet ball. The ball has a hole in it and the idea is to catch the ball with the stick.

Mexican children play with a wooden cup that has a handle on the bottom. The string has a small wooden ball on the end. The children try to toss the ball and catch it in the wooden cup. Usually it bounces out. If you want to make the Mexican version of this skill game, here's how:

1. Get a small tin can about 2 inches high and 1-1/2 inches in diameter (potted meats or Vienna sausages come in cans this size).
2. From your dad's scrap lumber, find a piece of wood that is square with about 3/4-inch sides. Carve the wood into a rounded handle.
3. Drive a small nail into the bottom of the can (at the center) and into the handle. Be careful not to split the handle.
4. Tie on string and a small wooden ball. Decorate the can and handle any way you like.

WINDMILL □ Holland

Holland is a tiny, flat country in northwestern Europe. Windmills dot the land near the many canals that run from town to town. Big water birds called storks perch on the windmills and houses. Dutch children play a game in which leaders called storks imitate windmills. Team members who fail to follow their leader often end up in the canal (a sort of jail).

The boys and girls elect a *berger* (in the illustration, he is standing at the left between the two teams). The *berger* then appoints two storks, or team leaders. The storks choose sides until all players are on one of the two teams. Each team should have an equal number of from four to ten players.

One stork draws a line on the ground. The second stork draws a parallel line approximately 16 feet away. The *berger* then draws a box at one end (see illustration). This box is called the canal.

Once the lines and the canal are drawn, the game begins. The players stand behind the line that their stork has drawn, facing one another. Each of the two storks stands slightly over the line. To begin with, the *berger* stands between the lines at the opposite end from the canal (see illustration).

Now the action starts. The storks begin to imitate either a windmill or a stork. Members of the teams must follow their leader. One leader may be flapping his arms like a flying stork, or standing on one leg. The other leader may weave from side to side, or move his arms like a windmill.

As soon as the game starts, the *berger* walks up and down anywhere between the two lines. He looks first to one side and then another, watching to see that the players imitate the motions of their stork. But when the *berger's* back is turned, the players can try not to follow their leader —without getting caught. When the *berger* finds a boy or girl not following his stork's motions, he dashes up and tags the player and shouts "Windmill!"

The tagged player immediately runs toward the canal. Everyone on both teams and the *berger* chase the player. If the tagged player reaches the canal before he is touched by anyone, he is safe. He returns to his place behind the line and the game starts again.

But if the runner is touched by a player from the other team, he must join that team behind its line. If he is touched first by the *berger*, the player must stay in the canal. The game goes on, even if a player is in the canal.

Once the *berger* has put a player in the canal, he usually watches the teams from near the canal. A jailed player is free when someone from either team slips past the *berger* and touches him. The freed prisoner returns to the line of the player who freed him. But if the *berger* touches a player trying to rescue a prisoner before he reaches the canal, the second player also becomes a prisoner.

When all players are in the canal—or on one side of one of the two lines—the *berger* says, "Windmill!" and runs. All players chase him. The player who catches the *berger* becomes the *berger* for the next game. The new *berger* selects two storks who choose new teams. And the game starts over.

BALANCING TOYS □ India

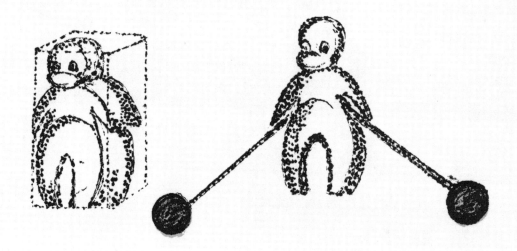

The children of India like to carve wood, and one of their favorite games is balancing carved animals—such as the monkey illustrated here.

Why don't you try to carve a monkey—or other animal—and see if you can balance it. First, take a piece of wood one inch by one inch by two or three inches, and sketch a design. Then, with a sharp knife or wood-carving set, carefully carve your animal. Balsa is easy to carve but soft pine is even better. An apple can be fun to use, too. You might even want to carve your monkey from a piece of soap.

Once the animal is carved, long dowels must be inserted in drilled holes and counterweights attached to the ends of the dowels. Lollipops sometimes can serve as the dowels and counterweights. Paint or stain the animal to your own taste.

For more instruction, see the drawings.

PASS THE ORANGE □ Ireland

An orange is most often used in this Irish team game, but anything that can be passed from chin to chin will do. That's right—chin to chin, no hands or elbows.

Two team leaders are selected. They in turn pick players for their sides. First one leader, then another, selects a player until everyone is on a team. If there is an extra player, he becomes the judge.

The two teams line up—with the leaders at one end. The leaders tuck oranges under their chins. At a signal from the judge, the leaders try to pass the oranges to the next player on their team. Each player must grasp the orange with his chin only.

This is a very difficult game. If the orange is dropped, it must be returned to the leader, who starts it again on its way. The team that passes the orange to the end of the line without dropping it is the winner.

HOLD THE ROPE □ Israel

Did you ever try to put on a hat without using your hands? This is a neat trick and a very, very difficult chore. Children in rural Israel play a team game. The team wins when each child gets his hat on his head without using his hands.

Players appoint captains who choose teammates. Usually there are a half dozen on each team. Two, three or more teams play at the same time—the more teams the more fun.

Each team has a home base. This base can be a line scratched into the ground or a circle. Each team has a length of rope long enough so that every member can grasp the rope with both hands. The teams' hats—one for each player—are tossed in a pile on the ground about 20 feet from home base.

At a signal each team grabs its rope and runs to the hats. That's where the fun begins. No one on a team may let go of the rope with either hand. Yet, somehow, each child on the team must end up with his own hat on his head.

The secret is teamwork; players may use knees, elbows, feet or teeth to help place a team member's hat where it belongs—on his head. In fact, any part of the body may be used to get heads and hats together, except the hands. A team that uses hands—or even drops the rope accidentally —is disqualified.

The team that makes it back to home base with hats on heads is the winner.

TUG O' WAR □ Korea

Over the centuries many different armies have invaded the land of Korea. At different times the Chinese, the Japanese and the Russians have tugged and pulled and made war in the valleys of this far-off country of eastern Asia. Despite the wars and the tugging, the Korean children—like children everywhere—continued to play their games. One of their games is a curious kind of Tug O' War, different because this game tests the strength of the individual as well as the team.

No special materials are needed, not even a rope. First the children choose sides. Usually there are at least four or five members on each team. Next a line is drawn, and the teams line up in single file and face each other.

The front players on each team step up to the line. The two players join hands and hold tight. Someone counts to three. At the word "three," each one tries to pull the other across the line. The one pulled over the line is the loser. He then becomes a member of the winner's team, and both go to the rear of the winner's line.

Once each pair of contestants has tested its strength, the teams line up again. Many players will not be on the team on which they started, and one team may have more players than the other. The players at the head of the line grasp hands again. The players behind the two grasping hands put their arms around the waist of the player in front. Then everyone pulls. The winning team must pull all members of the other team over the line.

STICK GAMES □ New Zealand

When European sailors first walked ashore on the lovely Pacific island of New Zealand, they were greeted by the warlike Maori tribesmen. These Polynesians were strong, handsome people. The Maoris in those days were cannibals. Today they are civilized, but they have retained much of their native culture, including their stick games.

Throwing and catching sticks is still a popular—and skillful—pastime. Boys and girls, and even men and women, practice this art. The sticks are often about 2 feet long, but they can be shorter.

Two or more players can play with sticks. Two players face each other. Each person has one stick. Slowly at first, the sticks are thrown simultaneously. The trick is to make sure that the sticks do not collide in mid-air. As the game progresses, the sticks are tossed faster and faster. The first player not to catch a stick loses.

Players may stand or sit or kneel. Usually the game is played while chanting songs. And sometimes the sticks are tossed so they deliberately touch. This provides a steady tap-tap rhythm. Throwing sticks makes young women more graceful in dancing and young men learn to be quick with their hands and eyes.

The game becomes even more difficult when each player has two sticks. The players then must be careful to toss the sticks while at the same time they are ready to catch the sticks the opponent is throwing.

When several pairs of players are tossing sticks, those who fail to catch a stick are out. The winner then tosses sticks with another winner. This continues until there is only a single player who has not missed a catch. He is the winner of the game.

CAT AND MICE □ Philippine Islands

Filipino boys and girls may be small, but they are often very quick with their hands. They are good at games that require quickness. This game pits a leader against several other players in a test of who is the quickest.

The leader is chosen. He is called the cat. The others are called mice. The mice sit in a small circle, surrounding the cat. The cat sits in the middle of the circle of mice. In a pile near the cat are some objects: stones, sticks, hats or anything the group agrees on. The mice try to steal these objects from the cat.

48

Everyone remains seated. Neither the cat nor the mice can walk around. The mice try to divert the attention of the cat and snatch an object and toss it over their shoulders before the cat can tag them.

If the mice get all the objects without being tagged, the game starts again. The cat player remains the same. But if the cat tags a player before he can toss an object over his shoulder, that mouse becomes the cat and they exchange places.

There are other variations of this game. It resembles the United States game of "Steal the Bacon," in which the players see who can get a single item and race back across a goal line.

HIT THE STONES □ Portugal

This is a game of skill and resembles bowling—in a rough way. Portuguese children usually do not have much money to spend on games. But the only materials needed here are stones.

First the players find nine flat stones and nine round stones. The round stones are placed on top of the flat stones. Then each player selects nine smaller rocks. These are throwing rocks that can be held in one hand.

The round stones on top of the flat ones may be set up in several ways (see illustrations). Whatever way they are set up, the first player tosses his small rocks, one at a time, from a line approximately 12 feet (more, if players are skillful) away from the stones.

The object is to knock the round stones from the flat ones. Once a player has completed his nine tosses, he counts one point for each round stone knocked off a flat stone. Then he sets up the stones as they were at the beginning, and the next player throws his stone.

Many children can play. The winner is the person who scores the most points in each game. This game may also be played as a team game, with alternate players from different teams throwing rocks. When one player of both teams has tossed his rocks, the team with the most points wins.

BELL IN THE STEEPLE □ Russia

Moscow, the capital city of Russia, has a long, cold winter. Snow covers the ground much of the time. Many of the games the children play involve a lot of running. One such game is Bell in the Steeple. Most of the boys and girls—and many can play this game—are on the move all of the time, running, dodging and chasing one another.

The only materials you need are a small bell (the smaller the better) and a box into which the bell will easily fit. Before the game starts, two players are chosen by the children. One is called the leader. The other is the guard who sits in the steeple.

What steeple? This is where imagination comes in. After the leader and guard are chosen, a big square is tramped in the snow. This big square represents a building. In the exact center of the big square goes a small square, called the steeple. Diagonal lines are tramped in the snow

(see illustration) from corner to corner, crossing in the middle and passing through the steeple.

The steeple guard takes the box and, holding it with both hands, steps inside the steeple. The players line up on all four sides of the big square, facing the steeple. As the guard hides his eyes, the leader hands the bell to one of the other players.

Now the game is ready to start. The leader takes his place on one of the four corners of the big square, and begins to walk. All of the other children follow him in single file. Around and around the big square they go, while the player with the bell rings it softly. The bell is passed from child to child, ringing all the time, while the guard watches closely from his steeple.

53

After the leader has gone around the big square once, twice or three times, he starts walking on the diagonal lines. The other players follow — still ringing the bell, still passing it up and down the line of players.

The guard suddenly claps his hands. All the players stop. They run toward the steeple and circle the guard. The player who now has the bell drops it into the box which the guard holds. And he runs. He may not run outside the lines of the big square. See diagram.

The guard, carrying the box with the bell inside, chases the player who put the bell in the box. And all the other children chase after the guard.

If the guard catches the player who put the bell in the box, this player becomes the guard for the next game.

But if one of the other players chasing the guard snatches the bell away from the guard, then the guard must chase the new player with the bell. This player may pass the bell to another player, and the guard continues to chase whoever is holding the bell. If the guard has not caught someone after several minutes of running, the leader can stop the game by running to the steeple. The person who has the bell then becomes the guard for the next game, and the old guard becomes the new leader.

HIT THE HOLES □ Saudi Arabia

Children in Saudi Arabia enjoy this special marble game. Each player has one marble. The children draw a line, and about 15 feet from this line, they dig a hole—not too deep—but about three or four inches wide. Five feet beyond this hole they dig another, and five feet beyond the second hole they scoop out a third.

Any number can play, but usually from two to six youngsters take part, with each individual pitted against all the others. Before the game starts, the players stand near the first hole and throw the marble toward the line. The player whose marble is nearest the line starts the game, and the others follow. The order of play is determined by whose marble is second closest to the line, third closest, and so on.

The first player steps to the line and shoots his marble toward the first hole. If he makes the hole, he puts his marble outside the hole and shoots toward the second hole. He keeps on until he misses a hole.

The second player can shoot at the first hole or at the first player's marble. Anyone who hits another marble during the game gets a second shot—as if he had made a hole. Each succeeding player has a slight advantage over those who shot first.

Once a player has landed his marble in all three holes, he turns around and shoots toward the middle hole, then the hole on the other end. Winner of the game is the player who has put his marble in 10 holes.

Teams of two also may play. In team play the winner is the team whose players both complete the 10 holes first.

NAME THE ANIMAL □ Switzerland

Snow sometimes lasts a long time in the valleys of Switzerland. Swiss children love to play in the snow. When they can't go out, perhaps because of a snowstorm, they play inside. This game is a good indoor game.

First the players choose a leader. He stands in front of the others with a ball (a sock filled with rags will do). They line up and face him. They

58

may either sit or stand, but all must do the same thing.

Tossing the ball up in the air, the leader appears to think. Suddenly he tosses the ball to the first player on his left, shouting: "Name the animal. The first letter is W."

The player catches the ball and tosses it back, saying: "Is it a wolf?" Or some other animal whose name starts with a W.

If the leader had a wolf in mind, the player who guessed right becomes leader. The old leader goes to the end of the line. But if the animal is not a wolf, then the first leader continues to toss the ball on down the line. If he gets through the line without anyone guessing the animal, the leader starts at the head of the line again, this time shouting: "Name the animal. The first letters are WR."

Eventually someone will guess that the leader actually is thinking of a wren (yes, birds are animals, so are fish). If the new leader wants to switch from animals to something else, he simply says, "Name the country" —or whatever he has in mind. And he tells the first letter of the country.

Many games are handed down from one generation of children to the next. And some move from one country to another. Turkish boys and girls play a game called Kukla, borrowed from Greece. In a way this game is similar to a favorite American game called "kick the can."

Instead of kicking the can, the players try to knock it over with beans or pebbles sewed into a bag. Each player must have his own beanbag.

First a line is drawn on the ground. The length of the line depends on the number of players. A second line, parallel to the first, is drawn 10 to 15 feet away. The first line is called the home line and the second the goal line. In the middle of the goal line a can is placed. A circle one foot in diameter is drawn around the can.

Each player, beanbag in hand, lines up behind the home line. In turn, everyone tosses his bag toward the goal line. The player whose bag is closest to the goal line becomes the guard. He stands behind the goal line. The remaining players again line up behind the home line.

These players toss their beanbags one at a time toward the can. The object is to knock the can over, and, if possible, to knock the can clear out of the circle.

Once the can is knocked over, the player runs quickly to retrieve his

KUKLA □ Turkey

beanbag. The guard grabs the can and sets it up again in the circle. Then he tries to tag the player whose bag knocked the can over.

If the guard tags the player before he passes the home line, the tagged player becomes the guard. The guard takes his place behind the home line, and the game continues.

Usually several players toss their bags at the can before one succeeds in knocking it over. Some of the bags land in front of the goal line, some behind it. When this occurs, all players who have tossed at the can and missed must also run toward the goal line as the can is knocked over.

Players whose bags are in front of the line must retrieve their bags and return to the home line. If one of them is caught, he becomes the guard. The players whose bags landed behind the goal line have a choice. They may grab their bags and return to the goal line. Or—if the guard is too close—they may stand in safety on their bags, and cannot be tagged by the guard. But they must stand on their bags until someone knocks the can over again. Then they pick up the bag and run for the home line.

When every player but one has been the guard, that person is the winner.

About the author-illustrator

Anita Benarde has had a varied art career. She has worked in oils, water color, inks, woodcuts and wood engraving. She has illustrated a number of children's books, among them **The River Spirits and the Mountain Demons, The Day the Indians Came,** and **The Bird Kingdom of the Maya,** as well as designing book jackets for numerous text and trade books.

Mrs. Benarde attended Brooklyn College, studied at the Art Students League in New York, and the Michigan State University School of Art. In addition, she has studied with Gertrude Hermes at the Central School of Art, London, where she developed new approaches to wood and lino cuts. She has also studied wood engraving with Stephen Martin. Her works are to be found in art collections both in the United States and abroad.

Mrs. Benarde is also a wife and mother. Her husband, a professor of Community Medicine at Hahnemann Medical College and Hospital, is an established author.

The Benardes make their home in Princeton, New Jersey, together with their three teen-age children and their dog Monster.

DATE DUE			